Value Investing

A Step by Step Guide to Getting into the Share Market and Making Money for the Long Term!

Table of Contents

Introduction

Congratulations on downloading *Value Investing: A Step by Step Guide to Getting into the Share Market and Making Money for the Long Term* and thank you for doing so. When it comes to investing successfully, it is extremely important to find the methodology that best suits your personal preferences. If you are interested in seeing reliable returns and extremely little risk, all while putting forward as little effort as possible, then value investing might be the right fit for you.

Unfortunately, it's not quite as easy as it seems which is why the following chapters will discuss everything you need to know in order to get started value investing as effectively as possible. First, you will learn all about why value investing makes sense regardless of how much capital you have to invest and why stocks, in general, are the most profitable place to put your money. You will then learn about the difference between price and value before learning about the importance of measuring performance. From there, you will learn all about the importance of understanding the business you are considering buying stock in, which includes learning how to read the accounting including details related to capital employed, operating income, cash flow, book value and shares, past and future performance, and shareholding friendliness.

Then you will learn about the importance of inexpensiveness and the ways price drives risk. You will then learn all about the ways in which you can keep your portfolio afloat in the long-term as well as other important endurance considerations. Finally, you will learn about just why preservation should be at the top of the list of things that all value investors care about.

There are plenty of books on this subject on the market, thanks again for choosing this one! Every effort was made to ensure it is full of as much useful information as possible, please enjoy!

Chapter 1: Value Investing Defined

While many stock investing strategies out there are exceedingly complicated, value investing relies on simple to understand concepts that anyone can use. It doesn't require a background in finance to use effectively or an understanding of technical analysis of any kind. Instead, if you have patience, money to invest and common sense, along with a willingness to learn, then you can follow the path of value investing greats like Warren Buffet.

In order to grasp the effectiveness of value investing, there are a few things you need to understand.

Every company has an intrinsic value: All of value investing can be summed up with an idea that most people learned at a very young age, you can save a substantial amount of money if you wait to buy things when they are on sale. While everyone understands that if you buy a television on sale you are getting the same bang for your buck as if you buy it at full price, most fail to see the fact that the same general principle applies to the stock market just as much as it does to consumer products. The only difference is that with the stock market it is the stock whose price is changing while the intrinsic value of the company remains the same.

Value investing creates a margin of safety: The margin of safety that is created when you buy stocks at value prices exists because you naturally have less to lose if the stock doesn't perform in the way you would like. This is one of the keys to value investing's effectiveness as it is naturally a significantly safer option than investing in speculative stocks which are likely to drop in price at the drop of a hat.

Value investors seek out stocks that they believe to currently be undervalued under the assumption that the price will eventually normalize as the market is bound to self-correct eventually. With this reasoning, the lowered price isn't the risk it is normally perceived as because the value investor has reason to believe that the price is currently experiencing little more than a slight downturn. For example, if you purchase a stock you believe to be undervalued at $66 and then watch it increase to what you believe to be the accurate valuation of $100 then you made $34 per share by simply waiting for the market to correct its error.

What's more, if the price climbs an additional $10 then you would have made $44 per share compared to the $10 you would have made per share if waited to buy the stock until the price had normalized. The father of value investing, a man by the name of Benjamin Graham, recommended buying stocks that were valued at a third higher than the current price. This is the margin of safety he recommended in order to earn the greatest returns while still minimizing the potential risk.

Ignore the Efficient-Market Hypothesis: The Efficient-Market Hypothesis states that the current price of a stock is the result of a wide confluence of factors, including accurate intrinsic value. Value investors believe that this is nonsense and that stocks are routinely overpriced just as they are underpriced. This can occur for a wide variety of reasons including things like how the economy is currently performing, investor panic or backlash because it was previously overpriced to name a few.

Chapter 2: Why Stocks?

Value investing is all about investing smarter not harder and that includes the security you choose to invest in. What follows are the main reasons that investing in stocks makes more sense than investing in other types of securities.

The Highest potential for growth: While the market has its ups and downs, as the Great Recession can attest, given a long enough timeline you are more likely to earn a greater return on your investment with stocks than you would with treasury notes, commodities, bonds and more. Historically speaking, stocks typically provide about a 10 percent return in the long-term compared to the 5 percent you can expect to see with Treasury bonds.

Currently, most savings accounts only offer .05 percent yearly interest on standard savings accounts. This means that if you have $10,000 sitting in your savings then you are seeing a whole $5 worth of growth each year. Without a doubt, there are better options out there for maximizing your savings and value investing is one of the safest bets there is.

Ultimate control: One of the keys to beating volatility and investing reliably is to control as much as you can through the use of diversification. Stocks, in turn, allow you the greatest level of freedom when it comes to putting your money where you believe it will do the most good at the moment. You will certainly want to have a portfolio that contains more diverse, and safer choices, but the more you keep in the stock market the more you will be able to easily control.

Time is on your side: Value investing is a type of long-term investment strategy which means that it is more likely to pay out in a big way the longer you leave it alone and let your investment grow. Having this extra time on your hands also ensure you will be more likely to profit because you will have the time to weather any downturns that may come your way. Risk and potential return go hand in hand and using stocks in a long-term investing scenario allows you to take on big risks in hope of equally sized returns.

The stock market is ambivalent: To the stock market, you are not a beautiful and unique snowflake with your own hopes and dreams, you are just numbers interacting with millions and millions of numbers, the same today as any other. While this might seem like a depressing thought, that is only because you are looking at it from a negative point of view. What this lack of personal attention really means is that with the right training, skills, and dedication, there is nothing stopping you from reaching your investment dreams and beyond. The only thing standing between you and that level of success is the time and effort you put into investing successfully.

Short and long-term value: Stocks are also unique because they can provide income in the short-term and growth in the long-term. Many value stocks that you come across are going to be what are known as growth stocks. As the name implies, growth stocks grow and then keep on growing. Once this rapid rate of growth ceases, so does the growth stock classification. If this is not seen as part of the lifecycle of a maturing stock then it typically leads to a hard backlash as well. Investors who are focused on growth are all about share price and pay very little attention to dividend potential for the stocks they invest in.

Income stocks, on the other hand, are stocks that represent shares of mature, stable companies that are more likely to pay out stable dividends. Dividends are a portion of a company's profits that are given back to shareholders, typically 4 times per year. There is also a special type of stock, called preferred stock, which pays a guaranteed dividend for as long as you hold it. If you are interested in supporting yourself solely on the stock market then a mix of growth stocks and income-producing stocks will ensure that you have all of your bases covered.

Chapter 3: Price and Value are Different?

As the great Warren Buffet once said, "Price is what you pay. Value is what you get." While for many everyday objects, the price of its item and the value are one in the same, this is not the case when it comes to stocks and their underlying companies. The coffee that most people stop for on their way to work in the morning, for example, has a price and a value of about $5 because that is what Starbucks convinced the world a cup of coffee was worth in the 90s. But that's the thing, prior to the rise of the modern coffee shop, coffee wasn't valued nearly as high as it is today so the price was much lower. As with stocks, coffee is only worth what people are willing to pay for it.

In the stock market, this fact is known as the difference between intrinsic value and market value. The intrinsic value of a stock is the value of the underlying company based on a wide variety of factors that are going to be discussed in later chapters. The market value is the measure of its worth on the open market as represented by what buyers are willing to buy its stock for. As long as the price of the stock moves in time with its perceived value, then the price of stocks works just the same as the price of coffee. When market value and intrinsic value are out of whack, however, is when the value investor strikes.

The trouble then comes along with the inherent level of difficulty that comes in determining the intrinsic value of a given company. As there are always going to be a vast number of variables involved, any of which could be rated as more or less important at any time, the estimates of the true value of a given company could possibly vary substantially between different analysts. Additional difficulties can arise from the material itself as a balance sheet, as it is created by an organization with a vested interest in a positive outcome, may not always be the most accurate source of information on a given company.

While some investors like to believe otherwise, the market value of a specific company is going to be reflected in its current stock price and will rarely reflect that company's true value completely accurately. This is due to the fact that the market value is always going to be somewhat distorted by supply and demand as well as overall investor opinion instead of purely based on the facts. While the fundamentals are always going to win out in the long run, supply and demand rule in the short-term which is what leads to the disparities that value investors look for. Market value is likely going to be greater than the intrinsic value if there is a strong level of demand, which can lead to overvaluation if left unchecked. The opposite will then be true if the demand for additional investment is relatively weak which can lead to undervaluation if an alternative trend isn't established.

In general, you will be able to get your bearings on a given company by looking at its earnings projections for the future as well as its current earnings and its historical earnings. It is also important to take into account market share, the current level of sales volume compared to historical levels and the strength of any competitors, reviewing analyst reports. Most of this analysis doesn't require any specialized training to interpret, it is largely about ensuring that the relevant numbers add up as they should.

On any given day, the market price of a given stock is going to be ruled by supply or demand. Factors that determine how a day will turn out include things like the prevailing market trends, relevant market news along with whether it is positive or negative, the general strength of the economy and the faith of investors that it will stay the same or improve and specific news from the company itself. As a general rule, investors are going to be more concerned with details that affect value and investors are going to be concerned with news related to the price which is another way that disparity is created.

Chapter 4: Measuring Performance THE BEST INVESTING MODEL

While correctly tracking the returns you see on your investments might seem like the first thing one would get in order before thinking about investing in a serious way, there is actually a good deal of disagreement around the topic which ensures it warrants additional discussion.

First and foremost, you are going to want to take advantage of measurements gleaned from historic performance. This type of data will help you to generate a baseline that can be used as a template to track returns moving forward. It will also make it easier for you to determine where you need to improve (if necessary). When making this assessment, it is important to keep it as truthful and straightforward as possible, it is not a contest, the only person you will hurt by being inaccurate is yourself.

In order to measure your own performance accurately, you are going to want to start by determining the percentage of returns you generated for the years in question. With those numbers in hand, you are going to want to determine the average rate and then compare that average to the standards you have previously determined.

When it comes to determining the return for a specific year, the first thing you are going to need to know is the amount of profit you generated compared to your total. You will then divide how much you made by how much you had overall to find a percentage related to your total returns for that particular year. Determining how much you made for a particular year can be decided by adding together four different amounts. The first of these is capital appreciation which is the amount the stock moved during the period of time, this will need to be done for each individual stock. If you owned the stock at the start of the year then you will need to subtract the beginning price for the year from the ending price from the previous year. If it is bought during the year instead, then you will subtract the purchase price from the price at the end of the year.

You will also need to factor in the realized gains which are similar to capital appreciation but for the stocks that you sold during the year. You will determine the price the same way you would the capital appreciation. You will also need to factor in the total dividends that were generated for the year in question, this number can be found on any brokerage statement. Finally, you will also need to factor in any interest that was generated during the year, this goes both for interest earned on cash received from stock that was sold during this period.

The result of adding all of these numbers together is then going to be divided by the amount of funds that were used throughout the year. It is this financial base that generates the type of capital appreciation, interest, dividends and realized gains you are looking for. This process will provide you with a more precise result than simply subtracting the start of the year from the end of the year. You can determine this number by adding together the total of any holdings that were carried into the new year along with the amount of any cash you used to purchase new stock during the year.

Dividing the first number by the second will provide you with your total return for the year. This number can be extremely useful as long as it is tallied accurately. In order to ensure that this is always the case, the first thing you will need to do is always include as much information as possible, if you have multiple accounts you are going to want to cover them all at once, even the ones that performed poorly. Additionally, it is important that you choose the right starting date and not choose a date that improves your overall results. If you don't include as much information as possible then you will be moving forward with partial information which can be dangerous for your investments.

With this done, you are also going to need to consider your yearly average rate as the average is going to tell you more than a simple return from a single year, especially when calculating your performance over the long-term. You should use at least three years' worth of returns when making this calculation. It is important to avoid using a standard mean when determining this amount as this type of equation will fail to account for the compounding effect of growth that makes investing so powerful.

Instead, you are going to want to use what is known as the geometric mean. Many spreadsheets are already capable of taking care of this calculation, just look for the function labeled geomean. Unfortunately, some spreadsheets won't be able to handle negative numbers, which is sure to come up from time to time. This problem can easily be avoided, however, if you simply add 100 percent to the negative result, perform the function and then subtract that 100 percent after the fact.

With this done you will then need to compare the average to the standard, of which you can choose either absolute or relative. The relative standard is a type of index. It can be found online. You will then want to take the geomean of the three years whose data you are comparing. This result will be your benchmark number, if you meet or exceed it then you are right on track, otherwise, you will need to reconsider your plan as a whole.

Chapter 5: Understanding the Business

When it comes to value investing successfully, one of the most important things you will ever learn is the difference between stocks that are currently undervalued and stocks that are just junk. In order to understand the difference, you are going to need to learn all about the sector of business that you plan on buying stocks in. While investing in different sectors of the market is ultimately recommended when it comes to maximizing diversification and a minimization of risk, early on it is recommended that you stick to one sector of the market so that you can learn as much about it as possible without having to split your focus. Focusing on one type of business will allow you to have the deeper understanding to pick the correct choice between a pair of stocks that both recently dropped 20 percent in price when one of them is now undervalued and the other is only getting started on a steep nosedive.

When value investing it is important to keep in mind that the stock is merely the means to an end which is partial ownership in a given company. This means you don't need to pay nearly as much attention to various external factors that affect day traders such as volatility or daily price fluctuations and can instead focus on the bigger picture. Factors like these are not actually inherent to the company which means their importance on the company's value, in the long run, is negligible.

In addition to understanding the ins and outs of the sector of the market you are considering investing in, it is also important to apply what is known as fundamental analysis to the companies you are looking at. Fundamental analysis can be split into two categories qualitative and quantitative. Factors that are quantitative are things like accounting records and tax returns which are discussed in detail in later chapters, and factors that are qualitative are more ephemeral such as name recognition and the quality of its leadership. Before you make any investments towards your future it is important to take a look at each with equal interest.

For example, if you were to look at the qualitative factors of the Coca-Cola Company you would want to take into account its general brand recognition, which transforms it from a company that just sells carbonated water to a branding and marketing giant that is known literally worldwide. While this level of brand recognition cannot be accurately given a dollar amount, it is clearly one of the major contributing factors to the company's continued success.

Important qualitative factors to consider

Business model: The first thing that you are going to want to do when you catch wind of a company that might be worth following up on is to check out its business model which is more or less a generalization of how it makes its money. You can typically find these sorts of details on the company website or in its 10-K filing.

Competitive advantage: It is also important to consider the various competitive advantages that the company you have your eye on might have over its competition. Companies that are going to be successful in the long-term are always going to have an advantage over their competition in one of two ways. They can either have better operational effectiveness or improved strategic positioning. Operational effectiveness is the name given to doing the same things as the competition but in a more efficient and effective way. Strategic positioning occurs when a company gains an edge by doing things that nobody else is doing.

Leadership: The type of management that is currently leading a company is going to go a long way towards determining if it is going to be successful in the long run. After all, even the most well thought out business plan will fail without being able to rely on the right infrastructure to support it in the long run. When it comes to analyzing management, the first place you are going to want to look is the corporate information section of the company's website. This won't provide you with much more than the names of the folks at the top, but if they have been around the block then names should be enough to pull up everything you need to know about their past work experiences. While this might not ultimately amount to much if there is something unfortunate in their past this should bring it to light.

Chapter 6: Reading the Accounting

Besides qualitative fundamental analysis, it is also important that you take a look at the financial side of things with quantitative fundamental analysis as well. While qualitative concepts are often open to interpretation, the financial documents a company provides will give you cold hard facts about how healthy the company truly is.

Documents to watch

Balance sheet: The company's balance sheet is going to show a variety of detailed records of the company's liabilities, assets, and equity for a specific period of time. In order to determine current assets, a balance sheet divides the equity of the company by a combination of liabilities and shareholders to determine the true financial structure of the company in question. Assets can include things like machinery, buildings, cash, inventory and any other resources the company is currently in majority control of. The balance sheet will also determine the relative value of the financing that was required in order to generate the assets in question be it a liability or an asset. Liabilities typically denote a debt that must be paid back while equity represents money that controlling members have put into the company directly. Equity can all include profits from previous years and are referred to as retained earnings.

Income statement: If a balance sheet can be thought of as a snapshot of a company's economic fundamentals, then the income statement is a deep dive into a company's details for a specific timeframe. The most common income statements you are likely to come across are going to be either quarterly or annually. Income statements provide loads of useful information when it comes to things like revenue, profit, and expenses that were generated by the company for the timeframe in question.

Cash flow statement: As the name implies, a cash flow statement shows the full record of all of the money that passed through the company over a set period of time. Cash Flow statements typically focus on funds from several different places, starting with the operating cash flow which charts all day-to-day funds that are generated by general operations. It also tracks investment dollars and how they are spending along with funds that are generated from the sale of assets that the company previously held including things like large equipment or other holdings. Finally, funds due to financing are funds that are received or paid off based on borrowing or issuing funds.

The cash flow statement is definitely one to watch as it is much more difficult to manipulate than many other types of financial details. While accounts can certainly manipulate earnings, if they are so inclined, it is much more difficult to fake the funds that are in the company's accounts. As such, many value investors consider the cash flow statement the most reliable metric when it comes to a company's current performance.

Tracking down the details

The SEC requires every company that is publicly traded via a major exchange to regularly file all of the documents outlined above. Additional information that is also required includes things like analysis and discussion by the management team, prospect and operations examinations, and auditor reports. To get a look at these types of details, you are going to want to track down a copy of the company's yearly 10-K filing as well as their 10-Q filings which are done quarterly. These documents can be found both online or in the real world.

Online, they can be found at the SEC's website (SEC.gov), though it requires use of the Electronic Data Gathering, Analysis and Retrieval system which was designed in the 90s, so learning to use its outdated interface is going to take some trial and error. Once you do track down the 10-K file that you are looking for you will see that in addition to financial statements for the previous year you will also have access to financial measures from a historical perspective along with various other pieces of information that help the company outline its current business operations. This typically includes things like risks the company is currently facing, plans for the future, number of employees, detailed management biographies and more. You may also run across the company's annual report, don't be fooled by it, the 10-

K will contain all the same information, just without the marketing spin.

Chapter 7: Capital Employed

Funds employed, more commonly known as capital employed, is the amount of capital a company has used to amass their current level of profits. It can be determined by finding the value of all of the assets that a business currently has and adding that amount to its working capital and fixed assets and by subtracting out any liabilities that are currently outstanding. A debt may be considered a current liability if it is going to be paid back during the next fiscal year; if it is a long-term loan, the current liability is the portion of it that will be paid back in the next fiscal year.

Capital employed is primarily used as a means of determining the return on capital employed which is used as a metric for determining overall profitability. It shows how much earnings are generated per dollar spent by being compared to the net operating profit. It can be determined by taking the earnings of the company before taxes or interest are taken into account by employed capital.

Fixed assets: When it comes to determining the company's fixed assets, you will want to consider any tangible piece of property that is going to be in use when it comes to generating income for at least the next fiscal year. These types of assets are sometimes collectively known as plant. Real estate, equipment, quality furniture, and buildings are all fixed assets, as are certain types of intangible assets such as patents and trademarks as well.

Fixed asset information is important as it will make it easier for you to generate an accurate view of the company's total financial picture. It may be difficult to track down, however, as companies are known to use a wide variety of different methods of depreciating, recording and disposing of assets. This means you will need to closely study the financial statements of the company in order to determine exactly how the numbers got to their current location.

This is an important step as fixed assets slowly lose their value as they age and they are often expensed differently than other assets as they generate income in the long-term. Tangible assets experience depreciation and intangible assets experience amortization, but either way, a portion of their costs are typically expensed on a yearly basis. The value of the asset should decrease at about the same rate as this amount within the yearly balance sheet. The way the asset depreciates in value can cause the amount paid to differ from the current market value of what the asset could currently sell for. This is not the case for natural resources or land as they do not depreciate.

Working capital: Working capital can be thought of as the current measure of a company's financial health in the short-term along with its overall efficiency. It can be calculated with the following equation:

Working Capital = Current Assets - Current Liabilities

The working capital ratio which is the number of assets currently employed divided by current liabilities serves to determine if a company has an adequate supply of assets in the short-term to cover all of its liabilities. If the results are less than one then the company is currently working with a negative amount of capital which means they aren't financially solvent. Likewise, if the result is greater than 2, you will know that the company is not maximizing its potential and is currently sitting on lots of non-invested excess assets. An ideal ratio is generally considered to be somewhere between 1.2 and 1.9.

If the company has a declining working capital ratio over a prolonged period of time this is also going to be a warning sign that things are not as they should be. This could be an indicator that the company is having a hard time keeping is sales volume up and that its accounts receivable is only getting smaller. Working capital will also provide savvy investors with a general idea as to how efficiently the company is currently operating. For example, if the company has a lot of outstanding customer bills then they will be unable to pay their obligations which will manifest as an increase in working capital. This is caused by the company not operating its collections in an efficient manner. You can find differences in working capital by comparing periods to one another.

Chapter 8: Operating Income

Operating income, also known as Earnings Before Interest and Taxes or EBIT, is the overall measure of profitability that shows the likely amount of revenue that will turn into profit for a specific company. Operating income is an important piece of information about a company to know as it indirectly measures efficiency. The greater the company's operating income is, the more profitable its core business is likely to be.

Operating income can be determined by the following equation:

Operating Income = Revenue - Cost of Goods Sold, Labor, and other day-to-day expenses

It is important to understand just what expenses you are going to include and exclude when determining operating income. You are generally going to exclude income statement items that are not directly used for core business operations, nonrecurring items like one-time transactions, legal judgments or accounting changes, or interest expenses.

For example, assume a company had the following details:

Revenue: $1,000,000
Cost of Goods Sold: $500,000
Labor: $250,000

Administrative and General Expenses: $50,000

Earnings Before Interest and Taxes: $200,000

Interest Expenses: $50,00

Earnings Before Income Taxes: $150,000

Income Taxes: $50,000

Net Income: $100,000

With this information in hand, you can then determine operating income by taking Operating Income = $1,000,000 - $500,000 - $250,000 - $50,000 for a total of $200,000. When it is written as a percentage of the overall sales, then operating income is referred to as the operating margin. In the above example, the company is making 20 cents for every dollar they make in sales.

There are several different things that can cause changes to operating income including labor costs, raw material prices or overall pricing strategy. As these types of items often directly related to management's day-to-day decision making, operating income can also then be thought of as a means to measure the overall flexibility of management and their competence when it comes to handling the unexpected.

Operating incomes also generates useful information when it comes to evaluating the operating performance of a company without dealing with tax rates and interest expenses. As these two variables are often going to dramatically vary between individual companies, removing them from the equation allows companies to compete on a playing field that is much more even that it would otherwise be. This type of analysis is especially important when it comes time to compare various companies in a single sector who vary in their tax environments or capital structures.

You will also need to keep in mind that various industries have a differing material and labor costs which is another mark in favor of comparing operating income or operating margins instead. This is also going to lead to a more meaningful comparison, though the definition of low or high ratio should also then be used in this context.

Cyclical companies: If a business is known to have an operating income that is sure to vacillate wildly depending on current market conditions then it is what is known as a cyclical company. Companies of these types tend to be creators of luxury items, home builders, hotel and resort companies, heavy equipment manufacturers, automobile makers, aluminum manufacturers and steel mills. This is not to say that these enterprises are not capable of making money for their shareholders in the long-run, getting there is just going to be a bumpier ride than with many other types of options. They are naturally going to see more contraction during times of economic downturn, so you are going to want to value them differently if you want to get the real scoop.

Chapter 9: Cash Flow

Cash flow is the measure of the funds that are going into and leaving a company's bank accounts. Free cash flow, a subset of regular cash flow, is the amount of cash that is left over once the company has paid any relevant expenses, along with whatever was spent on capital expenditures that were reinvested back into the company.

When you are looking to determine the free cash flow for a specific company, that information can be found in the cash flow statement that is part of the 10-K. With this information in hand, you are going to want to start with the operations based profits before locating any capital expenditures as well, these can be found in the investing section. You will then subtract the second number from the first to find the free cash flow.

If the free cash flow number is positive, then you know the company is currently generating an overall profit as it has more cash on hand than what is needed to both reinvest in the business and also run the company. If the free cash flow is negative then this shows that the company doesn't currently have enough cash on hand to support its business. It is common for smaller businesses to operate with a negative free cash flow as everything that comes in is immediately reinvested in the business.

Broadly speaking, the free cash flow is going to be similar to the overall earnings for the company with some of the adjustments that are typically made to an income statement. As such, you can often use the free cash flow number as a means of measuring the overall performance of the company in much the way that knowing their net income would. In fact, knowing the cash flow of the company, and its relating free cash flow yield is actually more useful when it comes to measuring performance than the P/E than the P/E ratio.

To determine the free cash flow yield amount you are going to want to divide the value of the company by the free cash flow. The resulting free cash flow yield will provide you with yet another way to measure a company's performance. The most commonly used formula is

(Free Cash Flow Yield = Free Cash Flow)/ Market Capitalization

When it comes to determining intrinsic value, finding the current free cash flow is a crucial step, specifically when it comes to determining the discounted cash flow (DCF). DCF is an intrinsic valuation methodology that will be extremely useful to you in all your value investing dealings. In order to determine the DCF, the first thing you will need to do is estimate the future cash flow that the company is going to have access to. Once you calculate the free cash flow and estimate it for the future year in question, you will then need to discount the results based on the current value in the present. This rate is extremely important as it represents the current time value of money. There are several ways in which this rate can be determined but the most commonly used one is the weighted average cost of the capital in question. With this in hand, you can then calculate the terminal value based on the future point that the free cash flow is being averaged from. The terminal value will also need to be discounted to the current value.

Having access to free cash flow information can help your value investing goals in several ways. First, the growth in the free cash flow that a company experiences in a single year is a great way to get a quick estimate of its overall health. You can also use the number to determine the free cash flow per share as a means of deciding it is likely that the company is going to offer dividends to investors. It is also a useful metric regardless if you are comparing similar companies or vastly different ones.

As a value investor, you are always going to want to be concerned with the question of the ways in which the current market value of a given company compares to its intrinsic value. The DCF over the entire life of a given company is a great way to find this intrinsic value. However, it is important to keep in mind that it is still going to be prone to all the issues that naturally come with forecasting a company's future. Choosing the right rate to discount the results to will also be an issue that will need to be approached carefully depending on your results.

It is also important to keep in mind that the free cash flow calculations tend to largely depend on the estimates that are being made and how accurate they ultimately end up being. Seeking out the operating cash flow can be a helpful way of arriving at a better idea of the company's true intrinsic value. The ultimate value that the analysis will have, and if any further action should then be taken is a decision that you will need to make for yourself when the time comes.

Chapter 10: Book Values and Shares

The book value, or net asset value in Europe, for a specific company, can be determined by looking at the sum total of its assets and subtracting out any intangible assets along with any potential liabilities. When you are looking to make an initial investment, you are going to want to look at the gross book value as well as the net book value which will deduct things like service charges and sales taxes.

The book value is useful as it can also easily be compared to the company's current market value to help you determine if the company's stock is currently over or underpriced. When you ultimately sell off the stock that you purchased via value investment, you will be able to determine your ultimate gains or losses by comparing the selling price to the book value.

The book value also allows you to determine the book value per common share. This is a useful metric as it allows you to determine the relative level of safety that each share you purchase in the company in question will have after any debts the company owes have been cleared. This is the current dollar amount that you would receive, per share, should the company liquidate today after all its debts had been settled.

The formula for doing so is: (Total Shareholder Equity –
Preferred Equity)/ Total Outstanding Shares = Book Value Per
Share

Book value gets its name from an old accounting practice of
recording the original, historical value of an asset in the books.
While the book value will then stay the same over time by this
measurement, the book value of the company as a whole will
increase over time as it accumulates new earnings through the
utilization of existing assets. As book value indicates the relative
worth of each share, comparing it to market value can work as
an effective means of valuation when it comes to determining if
the share price is accurately priced at the moment.

The book value per common share is going to naturally be based
on historical transactions. Subtracting preferred equity from
total shareholder equity reflects the amount of profit that was
earned by the company through the generation of stock and then
further enhanced by additional earnings or hampered by
significant losses. If dividends are paid by the company, that is
reflected here as well. If the company experienced a series of
stock repurchases at the current, improved, stock price then this
will also reduce the book value per share. Any buybacks of
stocks decrease both the common share count and the book
value.

The share total used for total outstanding shares is generally
going to be an average of all the common shares for the previous

year. It will also include additional shares that may be outside the basic share count, having been generated by preferred shares, stock options, warrants and similar convertible instruments.

There are naturally going to be limits to the accuracy of the book value when it is compared to the market worth of the shares if the market-to-market valuation is not used as well, especially when it is used on assets that are known to experience large swings in their market value. In cases like these, the historical cost book value would distort the true value given its current market price.

When dealing with the book value per share, it is important to understand how it differs from the market value per share. The market value per share reflects the stock price of the company in question at the moment which means it is what buyers are willing to pay for each common share. The book value per share, on the other hand, takes a historical viewpoint instead. When there are estimated increases coming to safety, growth or profitability market value per share will increase, regardless of what the book value per share says. As such, significantly different values can arise when the accounting principles used to determine each, vary on the importance of a specific point.

Chapter 11: Past Performance

Once you know what financial statements to look for, you will then be able to extract the right numbers out of them to allow you to generate performance metrics to determine if the company in question past performance is up to snuff.

Return on capital employed (ROCE): The ROCE is a percentage that indicates a ratio between operating income and capital employed. Essentially, it shows just how much money a business brought in compared to what it needed to bring in to ensure it could keep the lights on. The operating income number also denotes a specific period of time as it came from a specific income statement. Likewise, the capital employed describes a specific point in time because it comes from an individual balance sheet.

This is a crucial point as the capital employed can change substantially throughout the year as liabilities, cash balances and total assets will all be different at specific points throughout the year. As such, you have three choices when it comes to choosing the best time to consider. The first is at the start of the year by determining the capital employed from the ending balance sheet of the previous year. You can also look at the end of the year which entails using the ending balance sheet for the current year. Finally, you can also use an average between the two.

Free cash flow return on capital employed: This metric can be determined by taking free cash flow and dividing it by the amount of capital the company is currently employing. As with ROCE, this metric also requires you to pick a date on which to measure the rate of capital employed. Using the average of multiple dates typically makes the most sense. You will end up with a total of four different measures with this metric, each of which will be defined by the way time and cash are treated when measured. If the business you are measuring is currently experiencing a high rate of growth then this metric will be lower than the ROCE. This is due to the fact that cash flow typically lags behind operating income because it takes into account the normal cash cycle along with taxes and interest which operating income does not.

Growth in operating income per fully diluted share: This metric can be determined by dividing the operating income of the company in question by the diluted shares for the first two years. You will then want to subtract the first year from the second year and then divide the resulting number by the first year. The resulting percentage will give you the metric you are looking for. For example, if the operating income for a company, expressed as a diluted share was $3 one year and then $4 the next, the equation would be ($4-$3)/$3 or 33 percent.

Growth in book value per fully diluted share: To determine this metric you are going to take the book value of the fully diluted shares for both the first and second year before subtracting the first from the second and then dividing that number by the first. The resulting percentage will indicate how much increase in worth over the time in question based purely on the accounting numbers, though there is limited utility if you use it on its own. This is the case for a number of reasons, first, due to the fact that it doesn't take dividends into account as they typically come directly from the book value. As such, using them successfully means keeping that information available as well. This is also the case as this metric can be easily influenced by share repurchases as buybacks can cause this metric to return a false positive.

Growth in tangible book value per fully diluted share: To determine this metric you are going to take the book value of the fully diluted shares for both the first and second year before subtracting the first from the second and then dividing that number by the first. This metric can be useful, though it suffers from the same general limitations as the preceding metric.

Ratio of liabilities to equity: This metric can be determined by taking the total liabilities the company currently has by its book value. It is useful when it comes to determining the prominence of the obligations the company currently needs to deal with.

Chapter 12: Future Performance

Once you have determined if a company has been profitable in the past, the next thing you will need to do is ensure that it is likely to remain so in the future. While traditional accounting results will not be available, due to obvious limitations, strategic analysis can then be used in its place via a variety of qualitative tools.

Breadth analysis: This tool is used to determine the current breadth of the supplier and customer base and the likelihood of that changing anytime soon. You won't want to move forward with a value investment unless they are both looking good. You can generally assume that a customer base is significantly broad enough if no average customer makes up more than ten percent of the total client base. Likewise, a decent supplier base will be one where each supplier supplies no more than a tenth of all the operating expenses generated or goods sold. The exception to this rule is if a company has specifically focused on a smaller number of suppliers in an effort to maximize the discounts they get when buying in bulk. If this is the case then you will want to ensure that other vendors are standing by should current relations sour.

Analyzing the quality of the customer base can be a fairly straightforward process, but determining the quality of the current suppliers can be much more difficult as annual reports rarely supply these numbers. As such, you are going to need to make a list of the goods the business is going to need and then consider the branding, where the key components are sourced and what resources are required to construct them.

Force analysis: This tool generates an estimate of the prospective profits of a specific company. It is based on four different metrics, the weaker they are, the greater the likelihood of the company seeing an increase in profits. The first metric you are going to need to consider is the relative bargaining strength of the company's customers.

In general, the fewer the number of customers, the greater the power they are going to have over the company, which is something you will already know from determining customer breadth. You will also need to look at the ease with which customers can start doing the services the company provides themselves, the more specialized the company the less likely this is to occur. You will also need to take into account the costs the customer would have to take on in order to switch to a different provider of the goods or services the company provides. The more difficult it is for customers to go elsewhere, the less power they will naturally have when it comes to bargaining.

Likewise, it is equally important to consider the bargaining power that suppliers have over the company. As with customers, you are going to want to take the number of suppliers into account, and once again, the more the merrier. You will also want to take into account the ease with which the company could replace the vendor or internalize the services the vendor provides. The costs for switching vendors should also be considered.

Substitutes can come in one of three varieties. The first is via direct substitutions, where functionally identical products are sold by the competition. They can also come via the customer choosing to go without or to meet the same need with an alternative product or service instead. There are two primary things that keep substitutes low, one is the company's products are a better value and the second is the threat of high costs when faced with the prospect of going elsewhere.

It is also important to consider the industry the company is in and how difficult it is for new products to appear in the space. The harder it is for new companies to get their foot in the door, the weaker this potential threat is going to be.

In order for force analysis to be truly useful, it is crucial that you look at the forces that are in play for the company in question and determine if they are currently strong or weak. When it comes to utilizing force analysis, there is no middle ground, yes or no answers are required. If all of the forces are apparently weak, then you know that additional analysis of the company is likely required. If at least two of them are strong, then you are going to want to look the other way and never look back.

Chapter 13: Shareholding Friendliness

Assuming a company is still in the running after you look into its past and its future, then the next thing you are going to want to ensure is up to snuff is the company's level of shareholder friendliness. If a company is friendly towards its shareholders then it is going to have a history of generating a return for those who have invested in the company. This can also be thought of as the free cash flow that investors receive.

While there are several different indicators you can use when it comes to determining if a company is friendly towards its shareholders, these particular indicators don't have nearly as many easy qualifiers. Rather, the data for each needs to be collected and then analyzed as a whole before you can make a judgment based on everything that you have learned.

Compensation of ownership: The first thing you will need to consider is what the board members receive when it comes to their bonuses and incentives, along with their base salaries. Ideally, these will align with shareholder interests as much as you might reasonably expect which would include a reasonable salary for the executives and a partial salary for the time the board members do work for the company. The best-case scenario is also seeing them use their personal assets to invest heavily in the company, at fair market price, so that it constitutes a majority of their total investments. This is rarely actually the case, however, so the closer you can find to this paradigm the better.

Related-party transactions: A related-party transaction is any transaction between an individual that could pose a conflict of interest for the company. A good example of this would be if a board member owned one of the company's primary vendors. These types of transactions are only going to be an issue if it appears as though negotiations aren't taking place at arm's length. When you come across a scenario that appears to be a related-party transaction you are going to want to consider the frequency of such dealings, the amounts being dealt with and how opaque the entire process seems to be. If everything doesn't appear to add up to complete fair play across the board then you are better off looking elsewhere before you get trapped in a collapsing house of cards. You can find the type of details you are looking for by searching through proxy statements.

Share repurchases: While it can be easy to view companies purchasing back shares of their stock as a positive sign of trust in the future. This is only the case, however, if the shares are purchased at a value that has been discounted. Bargain buybacks benefit everyone and are beneficial when it comes to paying the tax man besides. This is because of the fact that when income increases in this way the gains that are seen by investors are untaxed. Likewise, repurchases at better rates are only useful to internal investors and can often prove destructive to the prosperity of the stock as a whole.

Dividends: While dividends are one of the classic examples of a company being shareholder friendly, this doesn't mean they don't come with a few drawbacks as well. First and foremost, dividends are taxable in a way that you, as the shareholder, have no control over which can actually make an ill-timed increase more trouble than its worth. Depending on when you bought into the company in the first place, dividends can actually be a sign that it may be time to move on as companies often only start paying out dividends when their growth opportunities begin to slow. If you bought into the company while it was young and on the rise and it has finally started paying out dividends then you will likely need to dig deeper into its future as it might be having trouble finding new projects that are likely to offer a high return.

Chapter 14: Inexpensiveness

As the term value investing implies, while having strong indicators is nice, a company is really only worth investing in if it is currently inexpensive. Expensive is a relative term, of course, but it is important to make sure that not only is a company priced below its market value, but that it is valued in such a way that it is worth investing in. This can be done by looking at a few key price metrics:

Times free cash flow: This can be determined by taking the market capitalization rate of the company in question and dividing it by that company's levered free cash flow. Levered free cash flow is just operations cash flow with capital expenditures factored in. Market capitalization is just the number of currently outstanding shares and should be quoted on the company's financial website. If not, you can find it yourself by taking the number of shares that were outstanding during the last 10-Q report and multiply that number by the price the stock is at currently.

Enterprise value to operating income: This metric can be found taking the enterprise value and dividing it by the operating income. In this case, operating income should be determined with capital exponentiations factored in. The enterprise value is what the company would be worth if it were to be the victim of a hostile takeover. The number includes the cost to buy all shares, not just all outstanding shares. This makes it somewhat difficult to determine because it is partially based on the current market price and it is also complicated to determine precisely. It can be found by adding the market cap to the market price of the company's assets and subtracting debts and minus cash. You should be able to find an estimated enterprise value on the corporate site, but if you are really considering a company you are going to want to look into it yourself as well, just in case.

Price to book: This metric can be determined by taking the market cap and dividing by the book value.

Price to tangible book value: It is the same as the price to book metric except that assets that are intangible aren't factored into the book value and trademarks, goodwill, and patents, along with other non-physical assets are removed from the calculation of the market cap. This can be a harsher metric to use than simple price to book but it can also be much more useful in specific situations. It is a better choice when it comes to analyzing companies that have grown dramatically via expensive acquisitions that might be propped up with too much goodwill.

Both metrics come up short when it comes to dealing with the distortion that occurs when repurchases come on the scene. While they both react to the same distortion, the results can vary between the two. If the price to book is strong but the price to tangible book value is even stronger then goodwill is often going to be quite strong as well. If this is the case then you are going to want to take a closer look at the company's previous acquisitions. Ideally, your results for the price to book are going to be no more than 8 and the enterprise value to operating income to be below 7. For reference, an enterprise value to operating income of 10 would mean that the market believes the operating earnings for the company will be at least one million dollars each year for the next one hundred years and that it deserves a ten percent discount rate. It could also mean that the market believes the operating income will grow at about four percent a year for the next one hundred years from the current one-million-dollar base which means it needs a fourteen percent discounted rate.

Chapter 15: Price Drives Risk

While buying a company for less is always going to be preferable to buying it for more, the fundamental reasons for doing so are at the heart of what makes value investing so effective. There are two main reasons that buying inexpensively is the most logical way to operate in the stock market. First, it ensures any returns that you do see are automatically going to be larger than if you did not follow a value investing strategy.

For example, if a stock that should be worth $4 is purchased at $2, then it is going to return one hundred percent of its investment cost. However, if you can purchase that same stock when it is at just $1 then you have tripled your returns. Buying inexpensively is also proven to lower risk, as you naturally have less riding on every single trade. If you become proficient at value investing then you can realistically expect to beat the return of investing in the S&P 500 on average, which sits at about 10 percent. Good value investors can expect up to a 15 percent return on their investment which is the number that should be your goal.

When it comes to measuring the risk of investing in stock in general, value investors are going to approach the market differently than other investors. That is, they look at it based on the chance that they are going to end up losing money. Value investors are naturally at odds with volatility, which is the measure that the price of a given stock is going to act erratically. While most investors see volatility as a measure of potential reward, value investors see it as a way of messing with a good thing.

Most investors view risk in terms of recent price fluctuations which, in and of itself has a number of problems. First and foremost, these fluctuations happened historically which doesn't necessarily indicate what is going to happen in the future. Stocks aren't precise in their movements which inherently means that any viewpoint regarding volatility is going to be based on faith which is not a reliable way to turn a profit. Additionally, the volatility view can lead to absurdities wherein the best course scenario, in theory, is different than what would actually work in the real world.

Value investing also contradicts another popular form of trading as well which is known as the risk-return tradeoff. This type of trading says that a good way to see improved returns is to generate enhanced levels of risk. This type of trading promotes angel investments, risky commodity funds and general risky investments that don't make sense in any other context. Value investing can be thought of as literally the opposite of this type of investment plan.

Chapter 16: Misjudgment and Misacting

While the primary steps to value investing successfully are understanding the company you are looking at, determining its quality and determining if it is a bargain, there are also three ancillary steps as well.

Knowing what to do: The first step is knowing what to do, which is easy if you find a company that is clearly profitable and currently undervalued but can be much more difficult if some aspect of the company is particularly arcane or if its profitability isn't as clear-cut as you like. While there is plenty of theory regarding what to do in a wide variety of situations, you will oftentimes still find yourself in situations where knowing the most straightforward solution is purely going to be a matter of experience.

Do it: While knowing the theory about what you are going to do in a given situation is one thing. Having the skill to put that knowledge into action when it is called for, is another thing entirely. It requires the decisiveness to not only determine the best course of action but to follow through on it when all the variables line up and you have a limited window when it comes to making a profit from all of your hard work. While taking advantage of a moment you have worked hard for might seem simple on paper if you haven't done it before, you might find it to be extremely difficult to pull off successfully. It requires a serious commitment of capital to a company whose stock is currently down and that most investors want little if anything to do with. Doing so successfully requires utter faith in yourself and a natural contrarian mindset that requires plenty of practice to solidify.

Don't do anything else: This step can be even more difficult for many people than actually committing to value investing for the first time. Once you have committed to an investment, then all that is left to do is wait. Value investing is all about the long-term which means that a majority of what you are going to be doing is sitting around and occasionally checking in on your investments in order to ensure that everything is proceeding as it should. There are no magic buttons you can press to make the process proceed more quickly and there is absolutely nothing you can personally do about any of it. If this sounds great to you then value investing might be the right type of investing for you, if it sounds like pure torture then something more active is likely going to be your speed.

Cognitive Biases

Additionally, when it comes to value investing successfully, it is important to be aware of your personal instincts when it comes to trading, both for when they can help you and when they can harm you. Cognitive biases are incorrect snap judgments that your brain makes based on incorrect information it assimilated at a previous date. They can be extremely dangerous when it comes to value investing as they can cause you to make poor judgments without even realizing it. Keep the following common cognitive biases in mind and ensure they don't interfere with your investing.

Affinity: The affinity biases suggests that purchase stock in a specific company because you like their products or their public image. While both of these might be enough to warrant a closer look at the company in question, it is far from enough to warrant actually considering buying into the company. Unless your reasoning for buying into a company involves cold, hard profit margins and low stock prices it isn't worth seriously considering. Be aware that affinity can also work in reverse, always consider every investment based solely on its own merits.

Reciprocity: This bias corresponds to the natural human tendency to base our current response to others based on the way they have responded to us in the past. It is important to always consider the quality of the information that you receive, regardless of the source. This will prevent reciprocity from affecting you either normally or in the inverse. It is equally important to never go ahead and make any value investment move until you have looked over everything yourself or had your own people look at the fine print. If things go wrong and you didn't take this easily manageable step then you will truly only have yourself to blame.

Anchoring: This bias occurs when you create a benchmark based on an inaccurate or irrelevant baseline. This bias is easy to fall into if you aren't looking out for it as it can be natural to want to buy when a price drops to a reasonable level. This is always going to be a poor choice, however, as the only real benchmark as to whether or not it is a good time to buy is the current price compared to the overall worth of the company in question.

Authority: This bias makes individuals more likely to consider investment ideas that are put forth by authority figures. Especially when you are starting out, it is important to avoid just following what the experts tell you. Not only will you make more money going against the grain, you won't learn the skills you need to be successful in the long run. While this route might lead to some small success, there are far greater opportunities out there if you only take the time to look for them.

Confirmation: This bias makes individuals more likely to take specific actions that already conform to their existing worldviews. While coming across a stock that is valued in a way that you believe it should be is a nice validation of your skills, this in no way implies that the underlying company shouldn't be vetted as thoroughly as any other. In fact, you would do well to look it over even more thoroughly than you otherwise might just to be sure that you aren't falling prey to this bias in the slightest.

Chapter 17: Portfolio and Selling

Once you have gone through the steps and found a stock that is worth investing in via the value investing method, a good rule of thumb is that you should invest ten percent of your portfolio into it, assuming a majority of your assets are currently unassigned. While there are certainly more complicated guidelines out there, this simple and practical metric should serve you well in most cases. While you might feel as though ten percent represents a lot of faith in a new company, sticking to this relatively high bar will ensure that you only make the type of investments that you truly believe in. If you don't believe in an investment wholeheartedly enough that you aren't willing to commit a reasonable portion of your investment capital then you are likely better off not investing at all.

Along with this level of confidence, it is important to keep in mind that if you are buying into the low on a stock it is unlikely that you are ever going to buy in at the absolutely lowest point. If you make the mistake of waiting for the best possible price then you are going to miss out on more viable deals than you will strike every single time. This leads to another reason to only ever put ten percent of your investment capital in one place, if you are wrong then you only lose a reasonable portion of your portfolio and still have more than enough left to rebuild successfully. It also ensures that you still have investment capital left over for new opportunities as they present themselves.

When it comes to managing a portfolio successfully, however, buying is only one-half of the equation, selling is just as important. Selling effectively comes with its own unique problems, the first of which is dealing with taxes. In most instances, any profit you see from your holdings is going to be taxable in one way or another. In order to ensure you pay the least amount of taxes possible, you are going to want to find the right value investments as quickly as possible and then hang on to them for as long as it is profitable to do so. The more you sell, the more you will ultimately end up paying in terms of capital gains taxes which means the less you will have to earn compound interest and the less you will have overall in the long run.

The other major problem that comes along with selling is replacing what you have sold. Ideal value investing candidates don't come along on a regular basis, and it is possible to go months without coming across a candidate that meets all of the required criteria. In general, if you don't have a new prospect lined up, you are best holding on to what you have for now.

Regardless, there are always going to be times when selling actually makes sense. One common instance when this is the case is if the price is dramatically higher than estimated value. If the result of the dividend of the estimated value divided by the operating income is greater than 25 than the profits you will make almost certainly justify selling. Alternately, if your initial evaluation proved to be wrong, then getting out before you lose anything else is likely going to be the right choice.

Another valid reason for selling is when the company is bought out by a third party. If this occurs then there is no telling how things might change for the prospects of the company in the short or the long-term. As long as things were proceeding fairly smoothly before the buyout then it is likely that the stock price is above the value so it should also be a profitable time to sell.

Finally, it might make sense to sell if you need the capital to fund a different investment whose potential for profit is going to dramatically exceed the current prospects. If you are considering this path, it is important to take a look at the new potential investment and ask yourself if you are really interested in it because the prospects are so much brighter or because it is something new and thus inherently full of more potential. If the new investment warrants the extra costs and hassles, then it may be worth moving forward on, but oftentimes this will turn out to not be the case after a closer examination.

Chapter 18: Endurance

When it comes to ensuring that you maximize your long-term investment potential it is important to hold onto winning picks for as long as you possibly can. One way to ensure you are able to do this as easily as possible is to ensure that your investment choices align with your personal morals. This peace of mind is crucial as otherwise you might someday find yourself in a crisis of conscience over a profitable investment and end up losing out because morals ended up winning out over financial solvency. As such, if you are planning to go the distance it can help to determine your general ethical disposition before you get in too deep.

Amorality: The first thing you are going to want to consider is how capable you are of viewing investment through a lens that excludes morality completely. If you are unsure of where you stand, consider how you feel about the sentiment that the ethical imperative of investing is growing wealth.

Moral failure abstention: The next thing you will need to consider is how you feel about investing in companies whose moral standing might be in question. Consider how you feel about investing in cigarette companies or those which make handguns to see where you land on this scale.

Moral success affirmation: You will also consider how investing in companies with only positive characteristics is going to make you feel. For example, would you feel better about investing in solar energy than you would about investing in oil?

Moral activism: Consider how you feel about the idea of buying into a company with negative characteristics and then pushing for change from the inside. Most shares do come with voting rights of one sort or another, which means that if enough investors got together to demand it, a company would have to put forth measurable change.

When trying to decide where you fall on the scale, it is important to not try and use one of the four to the exclusion of the others as this defeats the purpose. Ideally, you will use all four to determine your personal stance on the companies that you plan on investing to allow yourself the luxury to not have to worry about such things when you have real money on the line at some point in the future. While it is true that moral standpoints can change over time, if you stick with companies that fall within the framework of the four concepts discussed above, then it is unlikely that you will stray from them anytime soon.

Chapter 19: Preservation

While it's clear that investing successfully means losing out on money as frequently as possible, there is more to the reasoning behind acting conservatively than you might expect. To understand just why this is the case, consider a portfolio that experiences a loss of 50 percent in a single year, one that started in January with cash in hand, operated the portfolio throughout the year and then had half the amount they started with by the time December rolled around. Now, consider what all would be required for that investor to get back on the horse and try again.

In addition to the mental fortitude required to get over that kind of loss, they would need to experience a 100 percent return on all of their investments in the next 12 months, just to get back to where they were to start with. They would then need to experience another year of stellar returns just to break even, all from a single year's bad luck. Really stop and take a moment to consider this fact; investing isn't like other activities, if a mail carrier misses a day of work, they can go back the next day and continue delivering the mail without issue. If the mail operated on value investment standards then they would have to deliver twice as much mail the next day, in order to catch up.

This is the reason why value investors typically play it as safe as possible when it comes to moving forward with specific investments, the mathematics behind missed investments are punitive and there are no do-overs. If you do not put in enough time and effort when it comes to capital preservation, then your returns are going to suffer, it is as simple as that. Luckily, there are a few different practices that can help minimize these types of potential losses.

The first thing you are going to want to do is to consider every potential investment in three different ways. First, you are going to want to ensure it meets the three basics and is something that you know you should do and that you are capable of doing. Next, you are going to want to ensure that it is an investment actually worth moving forward on. Finally, you are going to want to look into the financials of the company and get to the heart of the matter.

The first two layers are always going to need to be addressed with every new potential investment but the specifics relating to the bottom layer will change based on the current situation. For starters, both general disclosure requirements and accounting standards will change over time, the longer you spend in the value investing game, the greater the likelihood that you need an update on the latest specifics.

Additionally, you are going to want to get in the habit of thinking in totals instead of dollar signs. If the amount you invested was low, then any amount that you lose will naturally be negligible, the system was designed that way on purpose. Just because the dollar amount lost was negligible, doesn't mean that a serious loss of 20 percent or more is something that you can expect to just gloss over. Thinking in terms of the percent of the whole will help to keep your investments in perspective. Getting into this habit early will make it easier to stick with it in the long-term after your individual investments become much pricier.

Gains follow this type of productive thinking do to the fact that investing based on value is naturally remunerative which is what keeps those who are successful at it coming back time and again. Value investing in the long-term has other positive benefits as well, the first of which is the fact that it can help you connect more fully to the world around you. All the stray bits of information that you pick up from day to day stop being meaningless static and start containing potential gold mines in the form of nuggets of useful information

Likewise, at its heart, value investing is essentially a truth-seeking exercise as it is all about tracking down facts wherever they may be. This is sure to be the kind of activity that naturally appeals to some people, regardless of the potential for financial remuneration it contains. If you like finding the truth regardless of the situation then you will find value investing inherently rewarding.

Value investing is also beneficial in that it rewards the type of long-term perspective that can ultimately apply to many of life's facets. With the results of value investing being so readily available, it is an easy way to see positive results from the practice which makes it even easier to develop into a habit that will see you through to the long-term. If you take the time to nurture it there is no telling what you might accomplish.

Finally, it can help clarify the fact that money really can't buy happiness and that after a certain point, net worth and happiness are not correlated in the slightest. No matter how much you might try and assure that this is not the case, money will never lead to the greatest joys in life. It can, however, allow you to experience them to the fullest as long as you utilize it correctly. Take the time you save by value investing successfully and use it to improve the time you spend with those you love, maximize your personal fitness and find ways to enjoy the life that doesn't have anything to do with valuation rates or operating interest. Investing gives you the ability to live your life to the fullest, take the opportunity to take what is proffered to you and enjoy every moment of it.

Conclusion

Thank you for making it through to the end of *Value Investing: A step by step guide to getting into the share market and making money for the long term!* Let's hope it was informative and able to provide you with all of the tools you need to achieve your goals, whatever it is that they may be. Just because you've finished this book doesn't mean there is nothing left to learn on the topic, expanding your horizons is the only way to find the mastery you seek.

It is important to understand that there is a difference between letting your stocks accumulate value and sitting around not doing anything. Just because you aren't actively moving your holdings about, doesn't mean you shouldn't stay up to date on the latest theories and practices in the value investing community, in addition to just what your investments are up to. The day that you decide to rest on your laurels is the day that you start running the risk of making the wrong decisions when it comes to maximizing your eventual payday.

Now it's time to stop thinking and start doing, the first step is one of the most difficult, but it can also be the one that is the most potentially rewarding. This is not to say that road to riches is going to be short, however, which is why it is crucial that you go ahead and ensure you have reasonable expectations when you are first starting out. Every facet of value investing is tuned to the long-term and if you give out mid-way through you are not likely to see much in exchange for all of your hard work. Never forget, value investing is a marathon, not a sprint, slow and steady wins the race.

Finally, if you found this book useful in any way, a review on Amazon is always appreciated!

Description

When it comes to investing successfully, it is extremely important to find the methodology that best suits your personal preferences. If you are interested in seeing reliable returns, and extremely little risk, all while putting forward as little effort as possible, then value investing might be the right fit for you. Likewise, if you are looking for an investment method that rewards patience, meticulous planning and an ability to go against the grain then *Value Investing: A Step by Step Guide to Getting into the Share Market and Making Money for the Long Term* is the book you have been waiting for.

While many stock investing strategies out there are exceedingly complicated, value investing relies on simple to understand concepts that anyone can use. It doesn't require a background in finance to use effectively or an understanding of technical analysis of any kind. Instead, if you have patience, money to invest, and common sense, along with a willingness to learn, then you can follow the path of value investing greats like Warren Buffet.

Inside, you will find everything you need to start value investing right away with a step by step guide that outlines everything you need to consider before buying stock in a particular company. The more you know, the greater your odds of success are going to be in the long-term and this book teaches you the questions you need to ask to find the types of stocks that are currently undervalued based on the true worth of the underlying company. Investing in the stock market successfully isn't rocket science, all you need is a low tolerance for risk and an idea of what details to look for when it comes to choosing the right moment to make a move, details you will find in abundance inside. So, what are you waiting for, take control of your financial future and buy this book today!

www.ingramcontent.com/pod-product-compliance
Lightning Source LLC
Chambersburg PA
CBHW071232220526
45468CB00002B/821